Classic Cars *of* Cuba

A TRAVEL PHOTO ART BOOK

LAINE CUNNINGHAM

Classic Cars of Cuba

A Travel Photo Art Book

Published by Sun Dogs Creations
Changing the World One Book at a Time
Print ISBN: 978-1-951389-21-5

Cover Image by Laine Cunningham
Cover Design by Angel Leya

Copyright © 2023 Laine Cunningham

All rights reserved. No part of this book may be reproduced in any form or by any means, electronic, mechanical, digital, photocopying or recording, except for the inclusion in a review, without permission in writing from the publisher.

Cuba's vintage cars have been called one of the most culturally stimulating aspects of the island. Some of these unique vehicles operate as colectivos, affordable shared taxis that follow set routes through Havana. A series of hand signals and a hundred or so Cuban Pesos are all that's needed to catch a ride.

For decades, the hundreds of thousands of autos imported during the first half of the Twentieth Century have kept running. Some have been meticulously restored. Others ended up with parts from different makes or models. More than a few rely on filler and creative metalworking to recreate their silhouettes.

Each vintage car tells of Cuba's history and its people. They are vibrant proof that passion and persistence can create something special.

HA!

CAT'S EYE

COWCATCHER

BELOVED

EURO

GILDED

FLY

COLECTIVO

DAISY

LUGNUT

SHARK

ZOOM

TWO-WAY

WHOOSH

SNUG

WAITING

FLARE

KICKING

ORCA

SEXY

TRIM

STABLE

SUNDIAL

VROOM

SNOUT

STRAIGHTFORWARD

SHADE

PUG

SHINE

ROCKET

HUMPBACK

CANDIED

STAR

WIDER

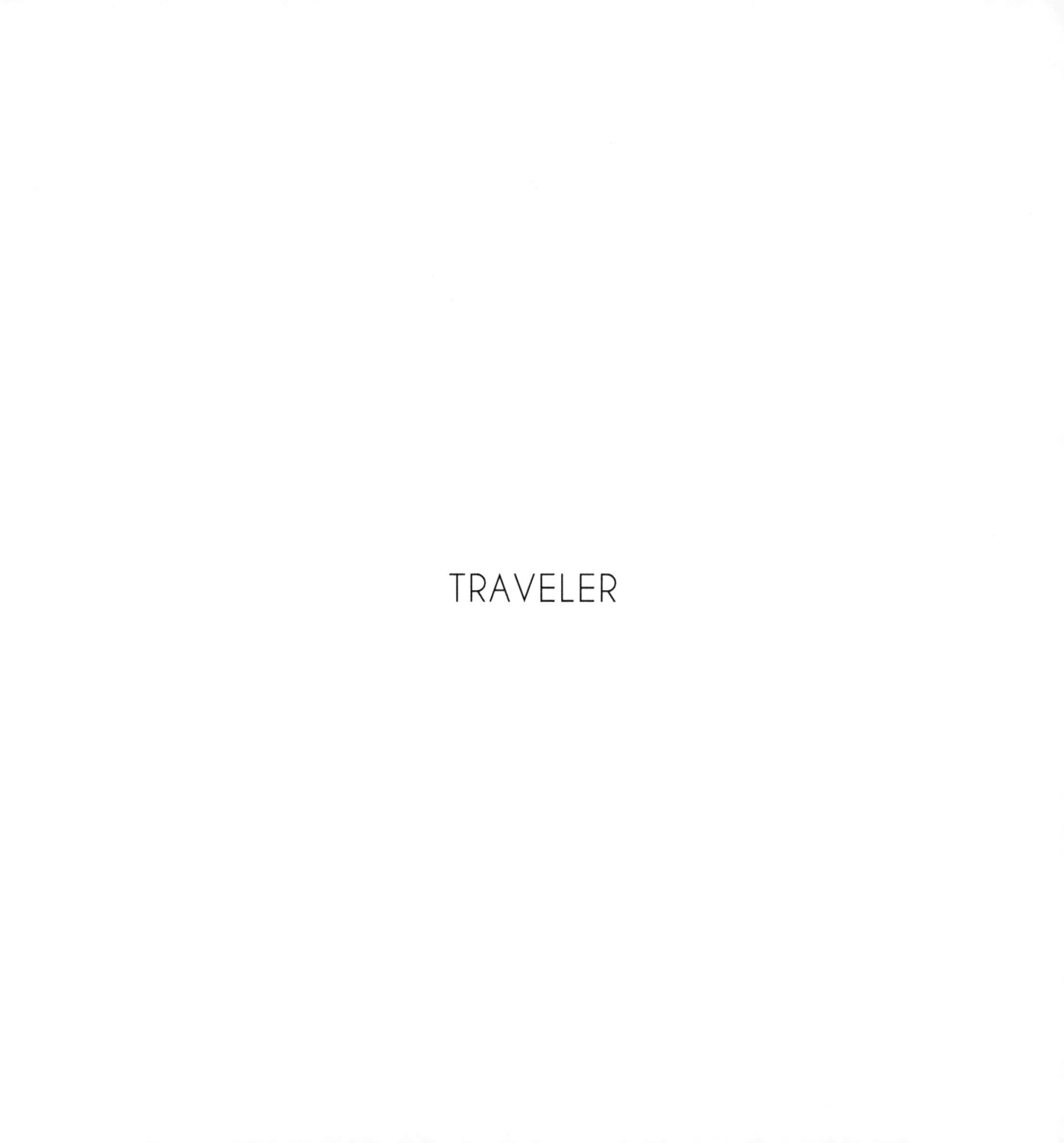

COMET

GROWL

POLLACK

ZIPPY

ALFALFA

RADIUS

SMOOTH

STARTING LINE

SOON

TITLES IN THIS SERIES

Havana, Cuba
Old Havana, Cuba
The Malecon, Havana, Cuba
Central Havana, Cuba
Vedado, Havana, Cuba
Regla, Havana, Cuba
Miramar, Havana, Cuba
Streets of Havana, Cuba
Classic Cars of Cuba
Classic Cars of Old Havana, Cuba
Classic Cars of Havana, Cuba
Spanish Colonial Havana, Cuba
Gardens of Havana, Cuba
Verge Gardens of Havana, Cuba
Cats of Havana, Cuba

www.ingramcontent.com/pod-product-compliance
Lightning Source LLC
Chambersburg PA
CBHW040001080526
44586CB00027B/2844